Smart Shark's Barmy Barge

Clive Gifford

illustrated by Simone Abel

Letts

M ark's Ark was the name of a safari park.
Visitors came from afar in large buses and cars.
They marvelled at the huge herds of animals.
And they rode on the safari water barge.
In charge of the barge was a park ranger called Mark.

People were scared by the wolf's snarl.
But they were all charmed by the animal farm.
And young kids loved to see the baby calf.

The star of Mark's Ark was not the wolf or the calf.
Wowing the crowds was the **super** Smart Shark.

Some words in this advert for Mark's Ark are missing a pair of letters. Can you complete the advert by putting **ar** or **er** in the correct spaces?

M_____k's _____k

Come to see the best saf_____i p_____k ev_____!

If you like birds, we have b_____n owls, l_____ks

and st_____lings.

If you like fish, we have p_____ch and c_____p

in a l_____ge h_____bour.

If you pref_____ animals on land, we off_____

a wolf and a calf.

And of course, our exp_____t rang_____s will show you

our sup_____ Sm_____t Sh_____k.

Visitors were charged large sums to see Smart Shark.
And they watched him perform his amazing tasks.
He used his fins to write and paint art.
After each task, he was served his favourite food –
sardine tart!

At dusk, Smart Shark
gave a concert in the park.
He was an expert on the guitar
and superb on the harp.
He could even sing verses
of opera, if people preferred.

"He is a **remarkable** shark!" people would marvel.
"He is the **cleverest** shark, ever!"
"You are a **star**, Smart Shark!"

The opposite of smart is stupid. List the words in the box with the same meaning as these opposites.

dull	clever	daft	wise	ignorant	brainy
dim	intelligent	slow	bright	dumb	quick

smart

stupid

_____   _____

_____   _____

_____   _____

_____   _____

_____   _____

When the visitors departed
in the buses and cars,
a strange change came over
the rangers in the park.

They stopped being kind
to the animal herds.
They teased the calf,
"We will carve you up for dinner
and add some herbs!"

They served the wolf
mouldy parsnips and barley.
"I cannot eat this food!"
snarled the wolf. "I am starving!"

By far the harshest
of them all, was Ranger Mark.
He had got a **scar** from
trying to harm Smart Shark.
Now he ordered the rangers to be
harsh to the wolf and calf.

But Smart Shark was planning
to have the last laugh.

6

Can you help the letters escape from their cages? Put them in the right order to spell the names of animals often found in zoos and safari parks.

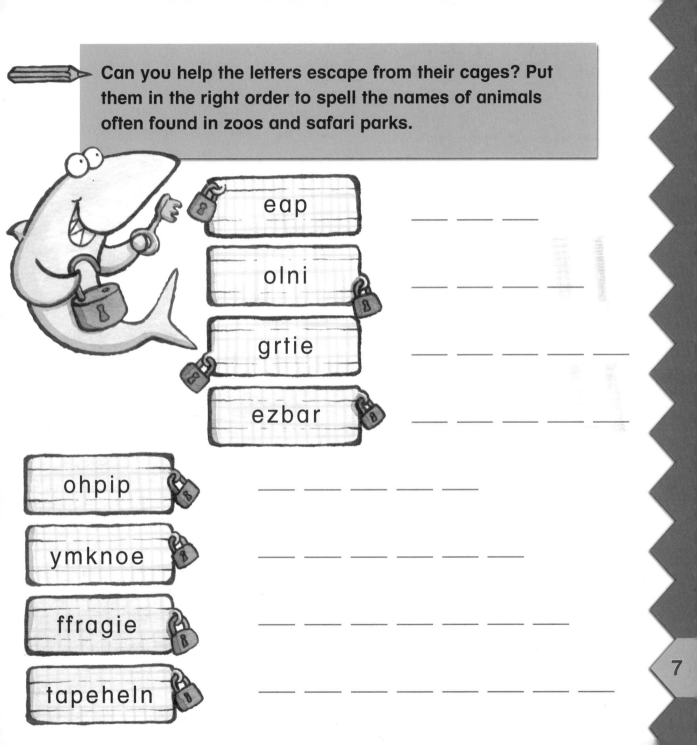

eap

_ _ _

olni

_ _ _ _

grtie

_ _ _ _ _

ezbar

_ _ _ _ _

ohpip

_ _ _ _ _

ymknoe

_ _ _ _ _ _

ffragie

_ _ _ _ _ _ _

tapeheln

_ _ _ _ _ _ _ _

Smart Shark called a secret meeting, one night after dark.
The wolf darted swiftly through the park.
He slipped past the rangers to join the calf and shark.

"Do you want to suffer living
at Mark's Ark?" asked Smart Shark.

"I do not," said the calf.
"I want to live on a real farm."

"I want to eat fresh food," said the wolf.
"I do not want to starve."

"Well then, my friends,
let us escape this harsh park,"
said Smart Shark.

"I have stolen the **KEY** to the harbour gates."

"How do we get to the harbour without alerting
the rangers?" asked the calf.

"Aha, I have made you ranger masks
from tree bark," said Smart Shark.

1. "He is a remarkable shark!" people would marvel.

2. I made this from old parts of my harps and guitars.

3. They marvelled at the huge herds of animals.

4. They served the wolf mouldy parsnips and barley.

5. He gave a scary snarl.

6. The startled man fell into the water.

7. The wolf and calf marched across the dark park.

8. "Hurrah, this is a great place to bask!"

The wolf and the calf put on their tree-bark masks.
"I am far too nervous to face danger," gasped the calf.

Smart Shark handed a toy bow and arrow to the calf.

"I made this from parts
of my old harps and guitars," he said.
"It will not harm anyone,
but now you will look the part!"

"Right, off to the safari harbour
to steal the barge," ordered Smart Shark.
"We can charge the barge past
the rangers and onto the river."

"Charge the barge out of the park? That is barmy!" barked the wolf.

The others looked alarmed as the calf started to laugh.

"We can do it! All aboard Smart Shark's **Barmy Barge!**" said the calf.

Can you write a short poem to tell part of the story of Smart Shark and his friends? You could use some of these pairs of rhyming words to help you.

harm
arm

shark
park

My poem _____

_____

_____

_____

_____

_____

_____

by _____

smart
part

barge
charge

harsh
marsh

So Smart Shark swam through the underground water pipes and the masked wolf and calf marched across the dark park. "Best to stay undercover and on our guard," said the wolf.

The wolf, calf and Smart Shark reached the safari harbour gates. Smart Shark unlocked the gates, and the wolf and calf boarded the barge.

The calf got the barge to start while the wolf kept guard.

"Darn it!" hissed Smart Shark.

An alert ranger charged towards the safari harbour.
He reached the barge,
but the wolf tore off his mask.
He gave a scary **snarl**
and the startled man fell into the water.

Can you fill in the missing letters to build the words? Read the clues to help you.

___ a r

something that is not near

a r ___

painting and drawing

___ a r ___

the opposite of light

___ a r ___ ___

the opposite of small

___ ___ a r ___

an item of woolly clothing

___ a r ___ ___

an event you might have on your birthday

___ a r ___ ___ ___

a package that comes through the post

___ ___ ___ ___ a r

a musical instrument

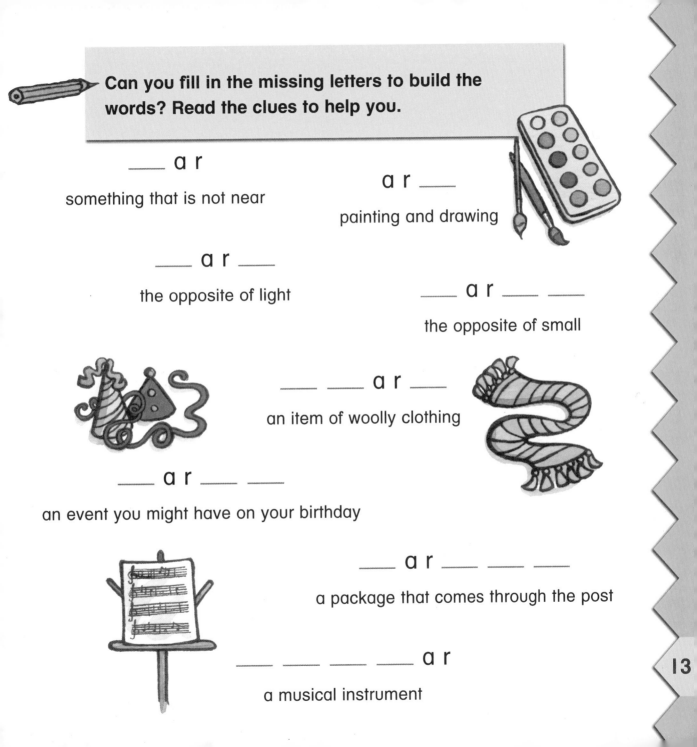

The calf and wolf steered the barge towards the river.
With Smart Shark pushing, the barge sped fast through the park.
"Hurrah for Smart Shark's Barmy Barge," cheered the calf.
"S h h h h . We do not want to alert more rangers," barked the wolf sternly.

But an alarm now rang out
all over Mark's Ark
and on the shore stood
a large group of rangers.

They barred the Barmy Barge's
path out of the safari park.

"We can swerve and dart through the
rangers' barrier," said the wolf.
"Keep your nerve and stay alert,"
warned Smart Shark.
"Wolf, full power...
Barmy Barge, CHARGE!"

To turn many words ending with **lf** into plurals, you remove the **f** and add **ves**.

Write out the plurals of these words, but watch out. One word does not follow this rule!

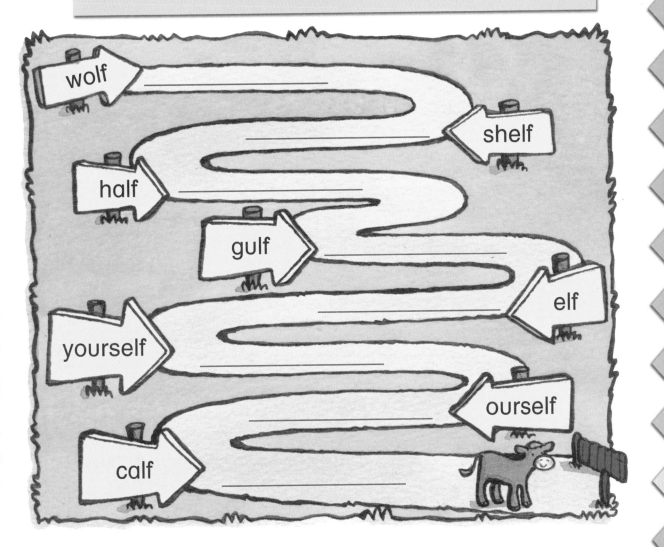

The barge charged forwards in the water.
The wolf snarled as he steered the barge.
It swerved and darted between the rangers' barrier.

Meanwhile, Smart Shark caught the rangers off-guard.
He arched his tail and jerked his fins
to splash them with water.

The barge blasted out of Mark's Ark and onto the river.
But it had not gone very far when the wolf looked alarmed.

"Smart Shark is still back in the safari park!"

"So you are not such a Smart Shark now!"
barked Ranger Mark.
Over the ranger's arm was a large net,
which could **trap** Smart Shark.

Can you work out whether each of the following sentences is written in the past, present or future tense?

 1. After each task, he was fed sardine tart. _____

2. "Hurrah, this is a great place to bask!" _____

3. The calf left first. _____

 4. I will make a new mask. _____

 5. We will take you to a farm. _____

 6. Smart Shark swam through the water gardens. _____

7. Here is your bow and arrow. _____

8. The wolf snarled and steered the barge. _____

Back on the barge, the calf grabbed his toy bow and arrow.
"I know it is a toy, but I must try to save Smart Shark."

Bang on target, the calf's arrow hit its mark.
The arrow's rubber sucker
stuck to Ranger Mark's arm.
It did him no harm, but it startled him
and he fell into the water too!

Smart Shark swam free and
joined his friends on the Barmy Barge.

"Free at last, thanks to Smart Shark!" cried the wolf.

"And thanks to you, wolf and calf, and our Barmy Barge!"

The barge swerved down the river away from Mark's Ark.
The three creatures were chanting, "Smart Shark's Barmy Barge!"

After the animals escaped, Ranger Mark gave an interview to the Daily Argus newspaper. Can you spot six things he said in the report that are not true?

Daily Argus

BARGE BREAK OUT

By S. Cape

"The animals in Mark's Ark are always treated very well. We always feed the wolf fresh food, for example. But then during the day, some of them attacked us with their claws and teeth, and with clubs. They left the park on a go-kart. Why am I wet? Oh I just took a hot shower." – Ranger Mark.

19

It was time for the crew of the Barmy Barge to part.
The calf darted off to eat grass and hay in a barn.
He joined the herd of cows at Garlic Farm.

After the calf had departed, the wolf turned to Smart Shark.
"Pardon me for saying your barge idea was barmy."

"It was a **daft** plan!" replied Smart Shark.
"But we all played our part!"

After the wolf had gone, Smart Shark swam on.
He swam past a river marsh and out into the sea.
"**HURRAH**, this is a great place to bask!"
"And what a lark to have escaped in the Barmy Barge!"

Now you know the story of Smart Shark and his escape from Mark's Ark, try answering these questions.

1. What did Smart Shark use to write and paint?

_____

2. What animal did kids love to see?

_____

3. What was Smart Shark fed every time he finished a task?

_____

4. What was the name of the harshest ranger at the park?

_____

5. Which animal came up with the name, Smart Shark's Barmy Barge?

_____

6. What were the wolf and the calf's masks made from?

_____

Answers

Page 3

Mark's Ark
Come to see the best safari
park ever!
If you like birds, we have barn
owls, larks and starlings.
If you like fish, we have perch
and carp in a large harbour.
If you prefer animals on land,
we offer a wolf and a calf.
And of course, our expert
rangers will show you our
super Smart Shark.

Page 5

smart: clever, wise,
brainy, intelligent,
bright, quick

stupid: dull, daft,
ignorant, dim, slow, dumb

Page 7

ape   hippo
lion   monkey
tiger   giraffe
zebra   elephant

Page 9

1. "He is a <u>remarkable</u> shark!" people
   would marvel.
2. I made this from <u>old</u> parts of my
   harps and guitars.
3. They marvelled at the <u>huge</u> herds
   of animals.
4. They served the wolf <u>mouldy</u> parsnips
   and barley.
5. He gave a <u>scary</u> snarl.
6. The <u>startled</u> man fell into the water.
7. The wolf and calf marched across the
   <u>dark</u> park.
8. "Hurrah, this is a <u>great</u> place to bask!"

Page 11

Many answers are possible. Check to see how many of the rhyming pairs are used in the poem.

Page 13

far	scarf
art	party
dark	parcel
large	guitar

page 15

wolf ➜ wolves
shelf ➜ shelves
half ➜ halves
gulf ➜ gulfs
elf ➜ elves
yourself ➜ yourselves
ourself ➜ ourselves
calf ➜ calves

Page 17

1. past	5. future
2. present	6. past
3. past	7. present
4. future	8. past

Page 19

Barge Break Out – By S. Cape

"The animals in Mark's Ark are <u>always treated very well</u>. We <u>always feed the wolf fresh food</u>, for example. But then <u>during the day</u>, some of them <u>attacked us with their claws and teeth, and with clubs</u>. <u>They left the park on a go-kart</u>. Why am I wet? <u>Oh I just took a hot shower</u>." – Ranger Mark

Page 21

1. his fins	4. Ranger Mark
2. the baby calf	5. the calf
3. sardine tart	6. tree bark

Published 2004
10 9 8 7 6 5 4 3 2

Letts Educational, The Chiswick Centre,
414 Chiswick High Road, London W4 5TF
Tel 020 8996 3333   Fax 020 8996 8390
Email mail@lettsed.co.uk
www.letts-education.com

Text, design and illustrations © Letts Educational Ltd 2004

Book Concept, Development and Series Editor:
Helen Jacobs, Publishing Director
Author: Clive Gifford
Book Design: 2idesign Ltd
Illustrations: Simone Abel, The Bright Agency

Letts Educational Limited is a division of Granada Learning.
Part of Granada plc.

British Library Cataloguing in Publication Data

A CIP record for this book is available from the British Library.

ISBN 1 84315 455 2

Printed in Italy

Colour reproduction by PDQ Digital Media Solutions Ltd, Bungay,
Suffolk NR35 1BY